Under the Sign of the Lily

The Messianic Sophianic Age

Open Up and Find Yourself
The Treasure Chest of My Existence

*The eternal word,
the One God, the Free Spirit,
speaks through Gabriele,
as through all the prophets of God—
Abraham, Job, Moses, Elijah, Isaiah,
Jesus of Nazareth,
the Christ of God*

Open Up and Find Yourself

The Treasure Chest of My Existence

*by Gabriele,
the prophetess and emissary of God*

Gabriele
Publishing House

The Free Universal Spirit is
the Teaching of the Love for God and Neighbor
toward People, Nature and the Animals

*"Open Up and Find Yourself
The Treasure Chest of My Existence"*

First Edition, April 2022
© Gabriele-Verlag Das Wort GmbH
Max-Braun-Str. 2, 97828 Marktheidenfeld
www.gabriele-verlag.com
www.gabriele-publishing-house.com

Translated from the original German title:
„Aufschlagen und sich finden.
Die Fundgrube meines Daseins"

The German edition is the work of reference
for all questions regarding the meaning of the contents

All decorative letters: © Gabriele-Verlag Das Wort
All rights reserved

Order No. S 334en

Printed by: KlarDruck GmbH, Marktheidenfeld, Germany

ISBN 978-3-96446-262-6

Open Up and Find Yourself

The Treasure Chest of My Existence

This small book is not a reference work. Nor should it be read page by page. It is a small guide for everyday life, for example, when worries, needs, problems, anger and the like hold us captive in our thoughts or when we have turned into a merry-go-round of feelings, pressing desires and persistent thoughts, when the same feelings, emotional desires and thoughts move us hour after hour, so that we can hardly call a halt to them.

This book is simply meant to be opened at random so that we may find ourselves on the page that beckons us today. Nothing happens by chance. Let yourself be guided! When you have worries and problems, but also when joy and harmony predominate in your earthly existence, take this little book in hand again and again. Let your consciousness choose the corresponding page. So that you do not influence yourself, you can close your eyes, in order to then open up to the page upon which you can find yourself today.

You should not merely read what is on the page chosen by your consciousness, but let it reverberate in you. This means that you should include it in contemplating your life, your thinking and wanting. What you read and include while contemplating your being will then begin to vibrate. The content of the words resonate with you, as it were. This is then a message for you.

Endeavor to now take in this message with your feelings, with your whole being, and feel into the thoughts that come up in you. From them, you can draw conclusions which will help you further on your path through life, which help you to help yourself, in order to remain healthy, to become healthy and to master your earthly existence happily and successfully. Therefore, learn to sense and figure yourself out, and experience that you are your own best teacher.

To have a joyful and happy life on Earth, it is important to always include the Commandments of God and the Sermon on the Mount of Jesus in your observations and reflections. The Ten Commandments of God and the Sermon on the Mount of Jesus are principles of the laws of the All, that ensure that the one who fulfills them step by step is on the best way. They find their way to their true self and gradually become free of worries, fears, needs, problems and much more. You become a freer and happier person who knows how to master the situations of your day, on the one hand, with the principles of the law of the All, which are simple rules of life, and on the other hand, through self-analysis with the question: Does my thinking and acting correspond to the Ten Commandments of God and to the Sermon on the Mount of Jesus? Those who take their life in hand in this awareness gain the help of the universal Spirit, in order to gain mastery over themselves, over their situations in life and over the stresses of the day. Those who work on themselves in this spirit begin to live.

The life is God, the eternal cosmic law of love. Those who take the steps into the law of love for God and neighbor become optimistic people who affirm in everything the life, which is God. They know how to deal with burgeoning fears, worries and problems. But they also know from where real help will be granted to them in illness and need.

The people who want to live happily and in peace must learn on themselves each day. They must learn to figure out their fears, worries and problems in depth, to analyze them, in order to find the root in their subconscious and in their soul, and to unearth it. Those who clear up the faults recognized, that is, what they have unearthed, who then no longer think and do the same and like things will not implant the same or like things in their soul either. This means that they will no longer sow them in the field of their subconscious and in their soul, and will thus become free from the everyday pressure of fears, worries and problems. These nuisances are the personal creations of the individual. They develop through wrong behavior, through behavior patterns that are contrary to the All-law, which is love.

We, every human being, are the creators of our nuisances. They develop from our impure feelings, thoughts and wishes—we are this ourselves, and none other. Another person can push and stimulate our weaknesses, but they can never implant them in us. Nor can they take them away from us.

Learning is always action. It is a daily process, because each day things come to us that want to tell us something, that is, they want to bring us a message. If we want to learn from what the day brings us, if we want to figure out the essential traits of our existence and develop principles from them, that is, values that are a part of our true life, then *we* have to do something, not the other one for us. What is essential for us is that from what we have recognized, our knowledge grows, and based on this, we change toward the positive, and our existence gains in quality of life. Spiritual knowledge without actualization fades away; it loses energy. Only the applied law of the All brings light into our soul and remains alive in us, until the body passes away and beyond that. Solely the fulfillment of the All-law gives us the feeling that we are gradually beginning to live.

If you do not simply let your fears, worries and problems, your hardships and much more stand undealt with or even fall into self-pity because of them, which always contains a few accusations of blame and guilt, but instead find your part in what moves you and rectify this, then—in your everyday life—a process of transformation will begin for you, which can be fascinating, if the "old Adam," with his fears, worries, problems and hardships, becomes a more life-affirming, glad, free and happy person.

I report from my own experience:
One day—after a blow of fate—I began to ask about life and to seek it. I asked my acquaintances the oddest questions. The content of each question had the purpose of learning about what life is and where it comes from. The one

answered: "As long as your heart beats, you are alive. After the last heartbeat, life is over." Another announced that for him life meant to experience nice hours, that is, to enjoy life and to take for himself what life gives. Still another said: "To live means to love," whereby he meant the corresponding body language. Another was of the opinion that life is a beneficial atmosphere; however, one needs money and possession in order to be able to afford this. Again another sighed and complained: "Ah, what's the point, anyway? I have tried out many things. With every high, I thought, now I am living. I felt well, I felt loved. I thought I was floating on a cloud. Some time later, everything was over again—hollow and empty like before. The cloud that I thought I was on shed its water and I was faced with reality again." His conclusion was: "To me, life means: What is beautiful disappears, just as I, too, will fade away."

One acquaintance touched my heart with his words. He said: "I read in a book that life should come from within. There is supposed to be something like a law of life." This answer triggered an "aha" effect in my heart. It was as if I finally got it. I thought: If life comes from within, then I have to now deal with two kinds of life, with the life that is outside and with the one that is inside and that should be the primary one. To reconcile these two "lives," the one within, and the other without, would certainly not be so easy.

I thought and dared and began to analyze my earthly existence. I found that my life, too, ran its course in an alternation of highs and lows. I got to the bottom of these movements and recognized that always when I thought, "now everything is good, my life is fulfilled," I got hit with a blow.

I continued to analyze and found that the external life is the materialistic life, which takes its course in pure ego. I thought and thought and came to the following recognition: The ego, which encompasses so many different egocentric patterns of behavior, cannot be the inner life, which should come from the source of the eternal Being and which—as it was explained to me—should be the All-law, which we call GOD. From this, I concluded that the materialistic, the external, life with its highs and lows, inconstant and deceptive, is thus merely a brief stay on this side of life, like an episode, in order to find the inner life, which must be exclusively God, constant and truthful, the eternally cosmic law of love.

I wanted to get to the bottom of the ego, which is always based on self-love and selfishness. As I continued to bring up the topic of "life" in my circle of acquaintances, at the end of the conversation one often came to the conclusion that life can be experienced in the love that is oriented to the body. But I realized that this is just as pleasure-seeking and possessive as any other ego, and that it is called "love" merely to mislead us about the many ignoble and morally base things that take place under this term.

It was soon clear to me that body-oriented love, or even physical love, has nothing in common with the All-love that I longed for in my heart. It fades just like everything else that briefly fascinates the person on an ego-trip. Physical love—as I became aware—is in most cases merely the drive for physical fulfillment, but not the life, not the love from the eternal source of Being.

Throughout all this thinking, so as to find the root of what life is, the firm and unshakable belief in the existence of God developed in me. From this, grew the certainty that all people have an immortal soul, which is an immortal being, because God is the God of life and God created and creates only life.

God is thus life. God is Creator. What God creates is eternal existence. In other words: If the life is in us, it follows that a part of us is eternal existence. And if God is *the life*, then nothing can exist anywhere in the universe, in the creation of God, where God, the life, would not be. The inner being, the life, the eternal, living existence, must therefore be all-encompassing.

Thus, the life can come only from within, and what comes from God is all-encompassing, consequently, also indivisible, because God is always the whole: indivisible life. I realized that, in the end, there can be no external life at all, otherwise, life would have to be divided into an inner and an outer life. From this, I came to the conclusion that our external human physical form is borne by the life, God. And why? So that as a human being we may find our way back to our origin, to our true being—which is *in* us, which God created, which God also maintains eternally—in the eternal life.

The longer I pondered upon all this and moved the recognitions in me, the clearer they became. The light of truth in them illuminated further aspects, and the inner horizon of my consciousness also grew ever wider. I felt a subtle joy in me, which said: Yes, it must be so, and so it is. Thus, everything makes good sense, and it also fits with the God, who is love, All-wisdom and kindness.

I was fascinated by the recognition that life is indivisible and that every person has an immortal being in themselves. We can also term this inner being as the child or the son or daughter of infinity, because we also call God, God-Father.

I continued with my analysis and self-exploration: If God is love, then God is *for* me, *for* all people, *for* everything that is. And this is why He gave us the Ten Commandments and sent us Jesus, who brought us the Sermon on the Mount, so that we human beings can practice step-by-step our way into the "for," into His laws, which are love. Thus, the "against" must be against the Ten Commandments of God, against the Sermon on the Mount of Jesus, against the laws of nature, in short, against the life. And who or what is against the life can consequently only be against God, who is the life.

I thought: Since the life, the divine, is in me, then each of my stirrings that is against the life—that is, against the Ten Commandments of God and the Sermon on the Mount of Jesus—is at the same time directed against myself. I am the originator as well as the receiver of my "for and against."

From this I concluded: If this is so, then I myself am the key and the lock of the "for and against," for or against the life. As a result, no other person can do something to me, only I myself, by being against the life.

Therefore, I myself contain what presently comprises "my life": on the one hand, the divine, the for, the potential of positive energy, and on the other hand, the against, the not-divine, the potential of negative energy, the opposing. If something negative comes toward me from without, then it hits me only when a corresponding negativity is also in me. The other one, who may have caused me suffering, is merely affecting my correspondence, the aspect or the aspects that are against God.

Those who create a negative energy potential in themselves—in their feelings, sensations, thoughts, words or actions—by inflicting harm on their fellow people or fellow creatures will, based on the cause that they have built up in themselves, experience corresponding things from others. This means that they will suffer harm, either of the very same kind or similar to what they did to others before. We call these correlations the law of cause and effect, the causal law.

Thus, causality means that the one who does unlawful things to others will, in turn, experience the same or similar things. Only one's own negativity gives another, whom we have tormented, the power to treat us accordingly. Therefore, the one who has an effect on our fears, worries, problems and needs, by tormenting us with them again and again, is only stirring the porridge of *our* causes, that is, stirring what *we* ourselves have created against the law of love, against the life.

I wrote down in a journal the many analyses and thought processes about life. I also noted down my "for and against," but also the victories that I had gained over myself. Soon my journal spurred me on to note down everything that moved me, that made me glad, my "for and against," my worries and problems, my analyses and much more. I recognized that a common thread of recognition went through my journal. Everything that I had recognized as negative and analyzed, whose root I had removed and cleared up and that I no longer did, brought me relief and a certain freedom.

Thus, I myself experienced that my thoughts about the "for and against" were in harmony with a higher truth, for it turned out that everything that weighed heavily on me and that I analyzed and overcame with the help of the mighty, eternal Spirit, paved the way for me, as it were, into ever more freedom, into ever greater inner joy. And not lastly, it brought me the certainty that things are as I had explored and recognized.

My journal became a loyal companion. I now regularly wrote down what was for, and what was against, during the day. I also made notes about my analyses, about how I cleared up my negativity and how I did things so as to no longer do this wrongful behavior.

When I first started my journal, I was at first very mistrustful of my own envisaged thoughts, about where life comes from and what life is. This is why I monitored myself and did it via my journal. I picked it up again and again and looked into it. I studied my notes and I saw my difficulties and hardships and learned how hard the analysis was for me at first, and how, in time, it became easier and easier. I sensed that I was being helped. Who helped me? The Spirit of the inner being, the Spirit of love, who is the life.

At first, I examined my notes every day, later, every week, then every month. I recognized the progress and was very happy about my "metamorphosis" from an anxious, worried type to a free person who *lives*. This gave me courage. I was happy about this. This inner happiness became a great eagerness, an incentive, to walk the path that led to the "for," to the "for life." My journal became my best guide. The many learning steps that I had made over the years made me recognize that my main task is not to look at the future, but at what is closest to me, in the now. This gave me ever more strength to do what I do completely.

Today I no longer need my journal. My conscience has become so alive that it nudges me every time inconsistencies come up. My conscience starts to analyze right away and immediately examines what is concealed behind everything, also behind the words and behavior patterns of my fellow people.
I myself became an open book. I have nothing more to hide. Everything that the law of the All, the great love and

wisdom, the life, wants to tell me vibrates into me; I become aware of it. This enables me to keep the law of the All-love.

Because I have become an open book, because I no longer nurture secrets and no longer belittle my fellow people, I see them as they truly are. I have learned to live in the day, in the present.
We human beings are in the habit of reviving our past—what we have not overcome—with our brooding and thinking. We do this by pondering over incidences and events, thus letting them come alive in our presence over and over again. By doing this, we unintentionally give power to, and again make current, what may have been behind us, like grief, blows of fate and the like. We can no longer

change what was. But we can analyze what causes us unrest, in order to find the root of what is preoccupying us, in order to clear it up, so that it then lies behind us as the past.

The more often we let the burdens of our past resurrect, the less we can recognize today, because we burden our life on Earth over and over again with the same thoughts of disappointment, bitterness, hatred and envy. Many people who day in and day out go round and round on the merry-go-round of envy, hate, of not forgiving and the like cannot recognize what the day wants to tell them today, and can master what lies behind them only with difficulty. The day then takes with it again the things, events and incidents that the person did not deal with—

things that it pointed out to them today and that were ready to be cleared up—in order to bring them once again, perhaps in a harder way. "Yesterday" is then "today," and today can become "tomorrow." "Tomorrow" can then be "yesterday" again, that is, the "past" renewed in future days.

This is how the merry-go-round turns and it turns ever faster with our thoughts. Our past becomes our present over and over again, however, of a more serious degree, and our life on Earth grows more loaded with blows of fate through our continued thinking and acting in the same way. If you want, examine where you stand. Open up to your page in this small book and you will find yourself therein.

May this small book become a small guide that leads you to the life, to happiness, freedom, health and peace. Who of us does not wish much, much life for ourselves? If you like, always carry this book with you. You will find yourself in it over and over again, if you want. And you will develop many positive powers—and gain very, very much.

Each new morning is a small incarnation, a small new birth. Thus, each new day is a piece of a new life. We decide what we make of this day, ourselves.

Our life on Earth is very precious. Take your life in hand!
Live in today! Never push your life into the future. Never say: "Tomorrow, or day after tomorrow or in a month, in a year, I will begin to live. Until then, I will have this or that cleared up."
Remember: Life is God, and God is the present. Therefore, life is today.

What does a day mean to you?

To me, each morning is like the piece of a new life. I awaken and am placed into a new day. To live means to make the best out of what it brings.

How does this happen? We do not let the hours and minutes simply pass us by, but we analyze again and again, what it means to be *for* the life or against the life. If we recognize negative aspects in the day, then we should dig out the root, carry out an in-depth cleansing and no longer do the same or like things. A conscious existence develops from this, from which the life comes forth. Thus, each day becomes becomes a piece of new life.

Measure your thinking and your entire behavior on the Commandments of God and on the Sermon on the Mount of Jesus. Then you will know at what level is the quality of your life.

We are fools when we simply vegetate away day after day and blame others for our existence, thus wasting our life. Through this, we squander the highest quality of life.

Life is harmony. Those who strive for harmony each day do not worry about tomorrow—they are consciously active and know that they are received by the life, which is God.

The one who constantly worries about the future suffers from nervousness, anxiety, a persecution complex, depression—all the way to the outbreak of an illness.

Among other things, a fulfilled life means to fulfill with enthusiasm the tasks the day brings to us.

The one who plans well gets more out of life.

Many people often plan months ahead. However, a good plan contains a good analysis. Those who make a good plan, in which possibilities are included in case some things need to be changed, and place their plan in God's hands while keeping their plan in their heart, can be sure that the great Spirit moves and radiates whatever needs to be taken care of today. If we are alert and recognize and do this, we sense that in our inner being we are greater than we ever thought.

Many people struggle through the days and always see in others only the enemy who wishes them misfortune. Self-torment does not lead to a solution, but the analysis of why we torment ourselves helps us to recognize ourselves. We have to find the root of the evil in us, dig it out and remedy it. Only this will bring calm and balance into our life.

Every person is their own personal enemy—not the other one who pesters them. The other one can treat them accordingly only if they allow this through their behavior against the law of life.

Realize that you cannot change your fellow people. You can change only yourself, that is, transform yourself.

A healthy mind is the prerequisite for a successful analysis.
Those who change themselves based on reason and on the analysis that comes of it contribute to a better environment. This means, however, that we do not keep our hands in our lap and merely refer to our experience.

A healthy reason can prevail, thus contributing to the analysis of our own reasons and abysmal depths, only when our conscience is still somewhat intact.

Reason can also be described as a scale between being opinionated and justice: Those who let reason prevail will not blame others, but will see their own part and analyze it, in order to then change themselves.

The others, no matter how they feel about us or act toward us, can always be like a sign pointing to the next higher step of reason and insight, when and if we want to recognize our part.

When blows of fate occur, many become fatalists, instead of fighting to find the causes and to overcome them with the help of God.

Let us not forget: The Kingdom of God, the Spirit of love, is in us. No person has enough energy to fight against fate and illness, but with the Spirit of the Christ of God, we can do it.

If you depend on the viewpoints and opinions of others, you are lost. Count on God!

A fellow person says: "I never lie; I can't even lie. Nevertheless, I cannot speak everything out, I cannot say everything. Because of this, I have to tell an untruth now and then—but I never consciously lie!"

It is possible that many a one does not lie consciously, but very often they deceive themselves and their fellow people, because they do not monitor what lies behind their words. A lie does not necessarily have to be the shell, the word—the content is what is decisive; in this, often lies the falsehood.

Those who do not know themselves, who do not figure out their feelings and thoughts will spread untruths.

If you want to find inner peace, then begin to create a good feeling of self-worth. Assess the content of your feeling, sensing, thinking, speaking and acting, that is, what lies behind your behavior patterns, and discard what does not correspond to a good character. Then you will also see your fellow people with the eyes of peace. You are the one who is called upon—and not your neighbor.

It is easier to tell others what they should do instead of first taking it to heart yourself. A good advice, given without your own actualization, often results in being tied to the neighbor. Their suffering then becomes our suffering.

Wrong thinking causes a dwindling of energy. The strongest weapon against this decrease in energy is reason. This brings about a proper analysis of one's own human behavior, which can lead, in turn, to recognitions and decisions from the heart.

Those who do not analyze their faults thoroughly and learn from them have, in the end, wasted their life on Earth.

Everyone dies, but not everyone who has died is dead.

The method for becoming happy is: Learn to recognize and understand yourself, then you will understand your fellow people as well. Those who have learned to understand themselves will also understand their neighbor more. This is a first step toward selfless love, the true love of neighbor.

If you want to become a good self-analyzer, then first—impartially and objectively!—gather facts about yourself, about your feelings, thoughts and ways of speaking, for example, why you speak and act the way you do. The "why" is decisive. From this come the facts, which you should then analytically break down, in order to find—in the first indications of the effects, like worries, problems, difficulties, fears and the like—the causes, that is, the roots, which should be rectified.

Remember the following:
A problem that is broken down is already half solved.

The one who does not learn to face the facts, to analyze them and then to make a decision that pleases God will never be happy. Their life will gradually become a burden for them. In old age they are then old.

In many situations, the word "experience" is only an excuse, in order to persist in one's own obstinacy. In many cases, experience is the key to turning the positive into the negative.

A hint for all those who do not want to make a decision that pleases God in their life in Earth: Those who want to age early should continue in the way they have until now.

Those who swim in a whirlpool of worries, fears and miseries still see only the fog. They do not live; they have become a product of their life and behavior. But God is life.

A piece of advice: How would it be if you were to try analyzing your problems and worries in time, in order to learn from them, on the one hand, and on the other hand, to discard what burdens you, instead of continuing to worry about it until the veils of fog are so thick that you escape into self-pity and illness.

Or do you want to become a master at revolving again and again in the same circle of problems and worries? Then stay with this and think about your problems and worries over and over again. At some point, you will end up in the middle of your circle, which will—often forcefully—give you no way out than to bear the effects or to go to the Spirit of the Christ of God, who is the center of the universe and also the center in you.

Thoughts of every kind—whether positive or negative—have an unimaginable power; their contents are magnets. The same contents of thought always attract the same contents, that is, powers, either of a positive or negative kind. Negative powers, negative magnets, are trapping stations in our subconscious. Positive powers are in communication with divine energies. They widen our heart. They are the all-powers of harmony.

With every negative thought, the human being goes against the life. Life can be attained only by living, not by thinking in terms of "for and against." Wrong thinking is a major weapon against the life.

Our earthly existence is often very sad because we worry about so-called "unlaid" eggs. An unlaid egg cannot have an aftertaste, because it has not yet been laid. But the one who becomes a laying battery by always thinking, speaking and doing the same things will also hatch his self-laid eggs.

Realize that you are the master of your thinking and acting. Take up the mastery of your thought and behavior patterns.

First change your attitude toward your neighbor, for each one of us also has positive sides. Orient yourself more to your neighbor's positive sides and do not make such a fuss over your personal ego. Those who have learned to think away from themselves have hardly any more time to think about themselves, their ego, or to think and talk negatively about others.

To realize means to gain self-experience, also in terms of the fact that people are and become what they think.

Those who take their life in hand begin to live, because they gain mastery over themselves.

Do not struggle with your neighbor in your thoughts and feelings, but with your own negativities, with your base nature, and resort to the Spirit of God for help to fight your baseness. Victory lies solely in you. It is the spirit of eternity, which will make you happy.

Therefore, fight with yourself to become happy. Happiness comes from the depths of your soul. It depends on you to clear everything away that stands before the gates to happiness.

If you believe in the good, then learn to be good from within! The Commandments of God and the Sermon on the Mount of Jesus help you with this.

Life is God. Happy is only the one who lives in God. The path to happiness means: Make others happy, then inner happiness will also move into your heart.

Inner happiness is an aspect of selfless love. Selfless love is giving, without expecting or even demanding anything in return. Those who give love will harvest love.

We should bring to mind more often that each one of us has to cultivate their own landscape—either well, less well or badly. Each one of us is their own landscape gardener.

Why do you eye your neighbors again and again, pass judgment over what they are, or want to dictate what they should do or not do? Think about the following: You are you, and I am I. Each one of us is unique in this world. We can become one in our hearts only by fulfilling the will of God, thus devoting ourselves to the cosmic All-law that formed us as divine beings.

Become the whole. This means: Become one with the core of being in your soul.

Are you also a brooder?
Realize the following: The earthly existence is too short to brood about trivial matters for very long.
Many people are in the habit of brooding and brooding. Some small thing is blown up and becomes a worry. We become anxious and nervous. Now it is time to give ourselves the command: Calm down and consider thoroughly what it is that you are worrying about.
Our fears and worries are often unfounded. However, if we keep on thinking about the same and similar things,

what we have imagined becomes a phantom formation of negative power. As a negative idea, as a thought form, it goes into our subconscious as a picture. By continuing to think in the same way, we intensify and vivify the evil. If it then has the necessary energy, it will control us and make us unhappy.

We should become accustomed to analyzing our worries in good time and to remedy them, before we fall apart on them.

A help for all those who indulge in self-doubt or in worries and troubles: You are stronger in your heart than you think!

Well, what do you have to say to this? There is only one who is to blame for your worries, your grief, your illness. And that is you, yourself.

Are you on an ego-trip?
If you are a person who bathes in self-pity from time to time, then read the following: Those who wallow in self-pity are on an ego-trip. The more often they wallow in the slough of self-pity, the more quickly they set themselves apart, because the others, who are not presently bathing in self-pity, do not know how to deal with them.

Anyone can change their negative attitude with an act of will, by aligning with God and finding God's will in the Ten Commandments and in the Sermon on the Mount of Jesus.

Never repay evil with evil.
For hate attracts hate; envy, envy; animosity, animosity. If we hate our enemy, then we bestow on them the power to rule over us, over our nerves, our health, over our senses and thoughts.

Hating makes one sick. Hatred is the tormenting spirit in our thoughts. It is we, ourselves.

Hatred poisons your organs depending on the degree of hatred. It can lead to heart trouble and stomach problems. Hatred can drive up your blood pressure, until you hear your heart beating in your head. Thus, venom can achieve many things.

A fit of rage can also affect the coronary artery. Such people poison their body depending on its magnitude.

Hatred, rage, anger and all addictions mark your face and your appearance. Your radiation is then grim and choleric. No plastic surgeon can smooth out these marks for long. No beautician can massage them away or make them disappear with make-up. Only you can rid yourself of them.

Hatred and addictions can also block your nervous system. But no one can force you to hate or to become addicted. You, yourself, build up these traits in your own feelings and thoughts.

Often self-will becomes a hobby-horse. The following statement can be helpful for the one who continues to ride it: If you want to become sick and susceptible to addiction come what may, then you have to continue thus.

Many objections can also be many excuses. An objection could be: "I cannot love my enemies."
How would it be if you were to bite the bullet, forgive your fellow people and see that what you get upset over or what has degenerated into hatred is a part of yourself that you have to clear up? Those who first work on the beam in their own eye, that is, on their part in a possibly

mutual animosity, will notice very soon that many a personal, that is, egocentric, spiteful thought dissolves as if automatically—unless behind this thought is a complex of the same or like thoughts. Then you have to work them off. Christ, the Spirit in your soul, helps you with this.

Change your way of feeling and thinking! In your inner being, clear up with your fellow people what you get upset about or what fans your hatred. Forgive and love the inner being of the person. From a spiritual point of view, the following can be said: This is the best medicine for your body and the relaxation for your nerves. Also for your face: Your complexion becomes rosier and your mood sunnier.

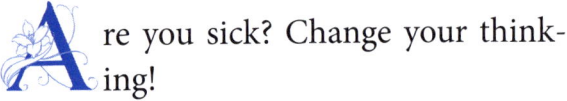re you sick? Change your thinking!

The content of your illness-producing thoughts, such as pressing desires, passions, brooding anxiety and much more are the originators of your illness. Realize: Positive thinking—that is, the contents of your thoughts and behavior that are pleasing to God—purify the subconscious and your body and contribute to your becoming healthy.

Break away from having the symptoms of your illness constantly in sight. Free, detached thoughts that are no longer permeated with fear and worry and bound with the heaviness of sinfulness are principles of the laws from the Ten Commandments of God and the Sermon on the Mount of Jesus. The step-by-step fulfillment of these inherent laws has an incredibly positive reaction on our nervous system and on our physical strength.

Every deficiency in the body, for example, pain and illness, works against the life, for the life knows no pain. Every pain, no matter how it manifests itself—whether in genuine pain or in the pain of self-pity—is thus directed against the life.

Let it be said to those who still think they have to get even with their enemies: This reckoning does not add up. Learn to love your enemies and love will return to you in happiness, health, equanimity and harmony.

Do you want to pay the high price of an early death? Then continue to create tension in your heart and in your nerves; drive up your blood pressure through hatred, envy, animosity, worry and anxiety—all the way to a heart attack. Your heart will then soon stop beating.

Many bathe in self-pity all too often. May the one who adheres to this read further: A bath in self-pity costs too many egotistical tears. You waste a lot of life force with this.
Save your energy for better things!

Become accustomed to breathing calmly and deeply. This is the best relaxation and it is lasting.

Perhaps today thoughts or situations will stimulate you to think about humility or humiliation. These two words—humility and humiliation—are in stark contrast to each other. Humility is of divine origin; humiliation is human. Become aware of the following reality: In the soul of every human being dwells the mighty Spirit, which many people call God. Those who turn within, in order to draw closer to God in humility and love, cannot be humiliated by any person.

Do you also think a lot about the ingratitude of your fellow people? Jesus advised us to first see the beam in our own eye. So, it would be better to first ask ourselves: Are *we* thankful?

Instead of concerning ourselves too much with why others are so ungrateful, we should get accustomed to thanking God more often, for example, for our health, for our well-being, for our family, the health of our children, our occupation and our work. There is much to be grateful for.

We could give thanks for joy and for sorrow, because in true gratitude lies greatness. Where there is real gratitude, there is also God's help in illness, hardship and suffering.

Those who think they have a right to gratitude and love will receive neither.

True gratitude is a sign of the refinement of character.

A piece of advice: Never expect gratitude, then you will never be disappointed.

Life is selfless giving.

Years ago, an acquaintance said to me: "Life is very complicated." I answered him: "It is not life that is complicated, but those who see all the things of life in the wrong light, because they are not satisfied with what they possess, instead always wanting to have more for themselves personally."

If we think away from ourselves and try to give without expecting gratitude, then we begin to live. But then, we also know what life means. Life is God and God makes one happy and satisfied. Every person who relies on God will become rich in their inner being.

Let us be glad for what we have and not always think about what we still want beyond this!

The cosmic law reads: What people let go of voluntarily is what they gain, and what they bind as a human being is what they leave behind with death. In all of infinity there is only one gain: the gain of life, and life is God.

We human beings want, want and want, thus becoming imitators. Many who do not attain what they have learned by watching others become unhappy. The end result is then worry, spitefulness and envy, because they did not get what they wanted.

We should realize daily that we are solely what our state of consciousness reveals. At every moment, every second, every minute and hour, we are what we once thought and think today.

A long time ago, an elderly woman said to me: "Most people deal with their worries as if they were the only ones in the world. If all people would put their worries tagged as crosses together in a pile and each one would look at the pile of crosses and place each one on his heart, then many a one would take up their cross again and carry it thankfully, because they have recognized: The crosses of others are often much heavier than their own."

Do you know yourself?

Many people are constantly seeking, because their longing to be different than what they are is not satisfied. If we know ourselves, then we can change ourselves at any time. However, without the effort to recognize who we are, we always want only to be different.

As long as we torment ourselves with the longing of wanting to be someone else, we will remain second or third class. If you want to find out who you really are, then become an explorer of your own person. Those who find their level of consciousness know where they must start in order to take steps in their life.

Why are we always having it out with others in our thoughts, when it is we who are closest to ourselves?!

Many people are in the habit of preoccupying themselves in their thoughts with their neighbors: why they are this way and not otherwise. If people would concern themselves more often with their mortality, then they might learn what the present means and what life means.

In all honesty: Don't we become spiritual wrecks with our frustration, with our worries and fears, with hate, despair, envy and annoyance? The resulting lack of energy enables pathogens to work their mischief in us. Then we usually visit a doctor who may prescribe a lot of medicine for us. In reality, this illness of ours lies in our soul; it is our spiritual condition.

Whether we are truly doing good will prove itself in the long run.

For many, the course of development turns into dependence! For example, those who have fallen into financial dependence should analyze why they are dependent. Those who change their attitude gain recognition. The right attitude is the door that leads into freedom.

Those who let themselves be dominated by people, let themselves be trapped by their surroundings. They then become a worker for the others.

Entrust yourself to the inner light. Become independent of the thinking and wanting of others.
Think positively! Do on your own what is possible and you will experience that an All-wise Spirit is the guide. If you attune yourself to the fulfillment of the cosmic laws, then your existence will be gainful—and perhaps a gain for many.

Many people confuse happiness with pleasure. However, true happiness is what comes from inner harmony. It is the cosmic harmony that is the life.

True life is happiness and true happiness is harmony.

If you are looking for the life, then change your attitude toward your existence! Life is wherever you look. It does not avoid the light, because life is light. If you look at the stars, for example—they do not retreat from the light, but are the light.

You, too, can become a star, which shines in the evening sky and gives light to all those who have learned to include the laws of heaven as a standard in their way of thinking and living.

Life is action. It knows no standstill. Life is the sole eternally existing energy, an eternally streaming power that knows neither dying nor death.

Place the power of the Spirit, God, the law of love, into everything that you think, say and do, by accompanying your words and deeds with positive feelings and thoughts. The result is that you will remain fit mentally and physically. Your body and your facial expressions will also look younger, because the eternal Spirit is able to stream through your soul and your body.

Learn to gain mastery over your body through the power of the Spirit, which is in everything, which can do everything. Only once you allow the Spirit, God, to stream through your body, will your body follow the Spirit willingly.

Learn to relax.

Sit upright, if possible, bolt upright. Place both feet on the floor. Place the backs of your hands on your thighs and draw them close to your body. Close your eyes and breathe deeply. Inhale all the way into your abdomen—and then slowly exhale.

When you inhale, your abdomen expands; when you exhale, you draw it in again.

Through conscious breathing, which you can practice several times a day, you will gradually gain distance from your pressing thoughts. You feel relaxed and strengthened.

Those who do these relaxation exercises often—if possible, now and then by an open window, in order to breathe in more oxygen and life force—will feel that their mind becomes more active. If we have gotten used to these exercises, we will soon realize that we also remain wide-awake and often retain the overall view and a grasp of the subject at hand during the most difficult conversations that can be very lengthy. This is because our spiritual consciousness makes an analysis, and through positive communication, points out possible solutions to us, so that the matter can be closed with a positive result.

These simple exercises of conscious, deep breathing lead to increased vigor and performance.

Live consciously, then you will retain your vigor into old age. Let the Spirit, God, become effective in you, by carrying out consciously everything that you do.

onscious eating is also a part of living consciously.

When you sit at the table to eat, assume again the upright sitting position already mentioned: Place both feet on the floor. Hold your body upright. Do not support your arms on the table; instead, take up the silverware consciously and eat slowly. Eat consciously. Chew slowly. Affirm the power of the Spirit in the food. Only once the body has taken in the food, take the next bite, chew it well and turn it over to your body. This results in an upright posture also when eating. Your breathing remains balanced; indeed, you breathe deeper.

The same thing is true with drinking. Drink in sips. Put your glass down while drinking, again and again. Do not simply let the liquid flow into your body. Taste the liquid; this is why you drink in sips.

The person who eats consciously also breathes vigorously and more deeply. Always remember that breath is life. A longer breathing rhythm may help you to have a long and healthy life, if your thoughts, words and actions are in accordance with the life, which is God.

Shallow breathing indicates that the person turns over many pointless thoughts and problems in his mind. He does not consciously breathe the divine power that begins to flow through positive communication. This results in the body becoming very quickly overtired. Such a person does not give the Spirit, God, the possibility to rule over his soul and also his body.

Correct breathing is the inflow of the breath of God, the life force. People who put their thoughts in order, who strengthen their faith in the Spirit—by fulfilling step by step the divine laws of infinity, which are love and unity—breathe deeper. They increase their life's vigor, because they detoxify their body by living consciously, which also includes breathing consciously.

Let us realize: The Spirit, God, is always young. Our body can be youthful right up into an advanced age, when it is an instrument of the Spirit that respirates soul and body and renews the cells, keeping them fresh and strong. Elderly people are no longer young, but they can be youthful through the Spirit, God, who is the eternal fountain of youth in the cellular tissues.

In every moment, in every second, in every minute, in every hour, each one of us is what they have made of themselves.

The life knows no excuse and no debtor. The life is impersonal, eternal Being without a cause.

If a person demonstrates "good deeds," this does not always mean that a good, that is, higher, moral lies behind them. For example, Some people think they do good deeds by repressing their tendency to egoism, hate, animosity, cruelty or lasciviousness. This repressed, that is, curbed, immoral aspect is covered over with "good deeds." The immoral aspect is, however, merely concealed. At some point, at the first opportunity, these tendencies will appear and many a tendency may have a stronger effect than it did years ago, because it takes energy to repress something. The immoral aspect attracts from the atmosphere negative energies that are the same or like it; it gradually intensifies and one day breaks out vehemently, possibly even massively. Many who today consider themselves to be a good person can be compared to a volcano that will surely erupt. Only the point in time is still uncertain.

When we look more closely, we see that those who wallow in self-pity are primarily egocentrics, because they always want to be at the center of important matters. If possible, the whole world should revolve around them and make them happy.

Melancholy is nothing more than feeling sorry for oneself with a strong attitude of accusation.

Many a melancholy person broods in their accusation about how they can take revenge against those who, as they believe, have brought them into "this situation." Melancholy can be cured only when those concerned realize that they themselves bears the responsibility for everything that they think and do, before God, before themselves and possibly before the worldly courts.

We will continue to stew in our "me and mine" until we have recognized our unimportance.

Some are preoccupied with how they can make trouble for another one, because they are against the other. Others are preoccupied with how to make their neighbor happy, in order to reap praise, and so it goes, always only me-me-me.

Which of the egoists is the "better" person? No one—because each wants something only for themselves.

Though our false thinking, we create a troop of armed forces that is directed against ourselves and thus, against the life. According to the content of our thoughts, we have created an army, the one more, the other less, that fights against the life and thus, also against our body.

Our conversations about illness, worries, miseries, problems and much more are the war cries of the enemy, whom we are ourselves.

Health and illness lie in our way of thinking and acting.

Who of us does not want to remain healthy or become healthy? Let us think about the fact that in health lies unity, the unity with our fellow people, the unity with our body. The cause of illness is a separation from unity.

Therefore, you yourself determine how you want to have it. Those who make peace with their neighbor gain peace in themselves. This change in our way of thinking leads to a constructive behavior of all the components of the body. However, those who always only worry about illness and health or other egocentric matters separate themselves from the unity. They think anxiously about themselves, thus thinking into their body suffering and possibly the separation from health, from the unity.

How would it be to not always brood about ourselves, but rather send friendly and loving thoughts to our fellow people, instead of seeing them only in the shadows of negativity. Realize that in each person is a mighty core of good, which is divine. Being whole and healing come about by thinking about unity, also with your fellow people.

Unity is based on the love for God and neighbor: Love your neighbor as you hope to be loved by God. Then unity will grow in you.

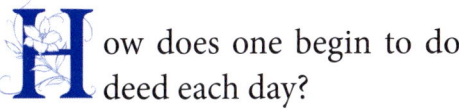

How does one begin to do a good deed each day?

By thinking about oneself less and less and being there more for one's neighbor. Those who use their days to this effect gain distance from their fears, worries and troubles. With the distance to their ego, they can analyze their former disruptive elements, their egotistical trivia, in order to find the root of the evil. If they remove this and no longer do the same and like things, they grow selfless and gain the life.

Happy are those who do not strive to accumulate wealth with every fiber of their thinking. Those who call great wealth their own and see in it the fulfillment and the good fortune of their earthly existence will one day have to learn self-denial and modesty.

Practice selfless giving!
If you have learned to no longer ask what you will get for your gifts or your help, then the inner happiness will move into your heart. Anxieties, distress and self-pity fade away.
The happiness that comes from giving love is victorious over every kind of hardness, every egoism, every expectation. It receives.

Arose cannot be transformed into a human being, just as the life cannot grow out of egotistical wanting.

The rose knows its fragrance. But human beings do not know their fragrance.

Many people suffer from their egoism.
Even though many a one is aware of the futility and emptiness of their egotistical existence, from which their behavior comes, many people run to psychiatrists, because their ego does not find the desired resonance and is not courted

accordingly. Many could help and heal themselves, if they would selflessly help their fellow people who need their help.
Those who think only of themselves become lonely and lose the communication with, that is, the access to, their fellow people.
Many people who find themselves on an ego-trip do not know what to do with their pointless existence and think that the psychiatrist should remove their sensory hallucinations about life and convey a meaningful life to them. In these consultations, "the others" are blamed in many ways for the loneliness and emptiness of their existence. Everyone who adheres to the idea that another is to blame continues to hang onto the sticky tape of their evil.

Every person has highs and lows in every phase of their life. Especially when we are in a spiritual low, we should turn to the inner source of strength that helps us to recognize the depth, the slant of our thoughts, to remedy them with the help of the Spirit, in order to thus rise up again, so that the sun of life will shine on us again, and we can take our next steps to the higher Being.

If you are on a low, then do not brood too long—turn to God in prayer! He helps you to figure out what you are brooding about, in order to remedy it.

Many people go through their earthly existence without perceiving their neighbors; they are like air for them. Only those who respect their fellow people regard them as their neighbors. And only those who have learned to recognize themselves also learn to understand their neighbor.

Those who belittle their neighbor need this.

No word as to what someone should or should not do, be it ever so well meant, has life force, if it not lived by us.

We will forget our worries and miseries when we think of our fellow people with love, instead of saying useless things about them.

Those who think only of themselves will not get very far in their life. And those who use their elbows to get ahead in life will have soon worn them out. If we want to get ahead in our brief earthly existence, that is, if we want to make progress, then we have to change our behavior, also toward our fellow people.

Those who do not fight against their hatred toward their so-called enemies, who are their fellow people, who do not repent of and clear up their spiteful aspects, but only ponder about how they can get even with them harm themselves more than their enemies.

Who are you?
You are the product of your thoughts. Learn not to imitate any person. Find yourself. Your all-too-human self and your true Self lie in you. The all-too-human self is in your thoughts; the true Self is the cosmic, impersonal thought that comes from your innermost being, which expects nothing,

which wants nothing, which gives without wanting to receive.

If you are happy that things go better for others than for you, then you are beginning to walk the path to God.

The human being should not reach for the stars by thinking he has to understand God. We can neither comprehend nor understand God with our intellect. But our heart can sense God's love, which is the power, the light, the stillness and the peace in all things.
We human beings can never fathom, never plumb the depths, of the mighty

Spirit of infinity with our intellect. If we believe that God is life and if we live according to the Commandments of God, then we feel in our hearts that God, the love, is present. Active faith in God, orienting ourselves to the Commandments of God and the Sermon on the Mount of Jesus brings inner security and joy. We begin to live.

Only God can make you happy, peaceful, healthy and balanced. He gives you the life; He keeps you alive. May I encourage you to revive your faith in God over and over again, through true, selfless acts of love for your neighbor?

The earthly existence is empty without active faith. Those who merely talk about faith and do not put it into practice with works of love for their neighbor indulge in self-adulation. Their existence becomes a farce.

Do you believe in a hell in the beyond?
If we take a look at our world, we do not need to puzzle about whether there is a hell in the beyond. The fires of hell are already burning in many ways on this side of life. The torments on this side of life, for example, with illnesses such as cancer, stomach problems, burns so terrible that the body is unrecognizable and

much more are enough so that we can say: We have hell already here on this side of life.

Who creates hell in this world? Who personally prepares hell for us? Neither God nor the doctors nor another. It is humankind that is constantly inflicting wounds on the planet Earth. It is each and every one who creates their own hell. How this looks for each one lies, in turn, in our behavior, which consists of the world of our thoughts, also of our talking and acting; for the five components of feeling, sensing, thinking, speaking and acting have their background, their content, which are decisive for the for and against in our life.

Who can lead us out of our hell? Solely Jesus, the Christ, our Redeemer. It is up to us to strengthen our faith in Jesus, the Christ, and to take the steps that He taught us. They arise from the Commandments of God and the Sermon on the Mount of Jesus. Those who walk the path to the Father with Christ have the power of infinity on their side.

Change your way of thinking by distancing yourself from thoughts that have as their content illness, worry, grief, hardship, hate, envy and animosity. Thus, let go of these thoughts. Strive to become a more trusting and hopeful person who thinks thoughts of health, freedom and happiness into their body and asks again and again for the help of the Christ of God.

Therefore, change your cast of mind, and your senses will refine. The great Spirit in you is the love. Health is the power of love. Say yes to the work of love that God wants to accomplish in you!

Every one is as old as they think and feel. The content of our thinking and feeling, which can be selfless or egocentric, is the chisel with which we have shaped our sculpture, human being. What people feel and think is what they express in their body.

Many a person who has reached old age could make the following objection: "My whole life long I have not worried about my thoughts and what they have as contents. The only thing that was important to me was that I attain what serves my well-being. I have remained healthy into my old age. I feel well."

To this, one can only say: It goes on after this earthly existence, for the life, which is God, knows no interruption. The cosmos is infinite and the patience of God is kindness, but also justice.

The material cosmos can be described as a large gristmill, in which the wheels turn according to the law of sowing and reaping. Because the material cosmos is large, it can be said that: The mills of cause and effect grind slowly. They allow each one a lot of time, so that they may attain many spiritual, heavenly values in their life. Those who do not want to do this will be hit today or tomorrow by what they have sown, for the mills of cause and effect also contain the wheel of reincarnation.

During your youth, gain your soul for yourself—which means: Live in such a way that the values in your existence come into accord with the innermost part of your soul and you will attain a rich, fulfilled life. Such a person will not age and become senile, but will become older in a youthful way.

Who does not want to be young or youthful? If you seriously want this, then think about the following:

Worries, problems, anxieties, grief, hate, insults or discord with one's neighbor make one weak and tired, possibly even sick and prematurely old. Powerful thoughts are affirming, positive thoughts that are in accord with the Commandments of God and the Sermon on the Mount of Jesus. They bring inner joy, inner happiness, the strength of faith, trust, security and they strengthen one's performance right into old age.

Begin to live during your youth, then you will affirm life and have joy in life in your old age.

If young people give the Spirit, God, the chance to gain mastery over their body, then later on, the elderly person is sprightly, flexible and healthy. Only the Spirit, God, keeps an older person upright.

Let us realize that a person's posture does not depend on their age. Those who already in their youth let their head hang down and go their way with creeping steps reveal in their posture their weariness and despondency, which are based on a wrong way of thinking and acting. Those who hold their head up straight and go their way with firm steps become calmer and stronger, because they breathe more deeply.

Those who affirm the Spirit, God, in their youth and take the steps toward the true life, which is the Spirit, God, will be affirming people in their old age, who uprightly and straightforwardly go their way to their goal, which is called life.

Concerning youth and age, the following statement of Jesus, the Christ, can help us: You will receive according to your faith.

The active faith is meant here; this means that it is decisive whether we are willing to recognize ourselves and that we change ourselves. Young people can already be old during their youth and elderly people can still be youthful during their old age. It always depends on our way of thinking and acting.

It is solely the eternal cosmic Spirit that makes a person noble and fine; it is not the person's body as such, that is noble and fine.
True beauty comes from within. Beauty is based on being pure and linked with God.

Those who treat themselves with care during their whole earthly existence, so that they will grow old, do not live. Life is spiritual activity.

May I convey a personal experience to you that comes from my active life? Those who treat themselves with care during their youth are old in their old age. Those who think they have to protect themselves in their old age also think falsely. The young person as well as the older person will not live longer by treating themselves with care, quite the contrary:

May the one who wants to rust, rest! They can shorten their life in this way.

Each of us is a tree of life, so to speak. Many people, many trees of life, set good fruits during their young years. Now it depends on us, how many of these fruits will attain ripeness.

To the youth:

What makes one elderly and old most quickly? It is the thoughts about the well-being of the body. Those who already worry about their body during their young years lose their youthfulness and are already "old" in their youth.

A piece of advice: Use the day and constantly look forward in the awareness that life-affirming and God-pleasing thoughts bring a good future.

No matter how old we are, the motto should be: Those who remain open for selfless thoughts, with an inner, alert awareness, fill their life with strength and initiative day in and day out.

Those who have kept their reason for reflecting and analyzing remain youthful. The life serves them, all the way into old age.

Those who base themselves on their so-called life experiences will become old already in the middle of their life on Earth, because they do not let reason, the power to critically observe oneself, have a chance.

To elderly people let it be said: Youth fades away, but youthful freshness can remain, if a person draws from the inner, spiritual wellsprings of eternal youth.

Those who earnestly and from their heart want to can even as an elderly or old person still change their deeply rooted programs of wrong thinking and acting, even negative, basic attitudes, into positive ones, by the step-by-step recognition of the causes, the roots, of their negativity, by clearing them up and consistently putting their way of thinking and acting into new, God-pleasing paths again and again.

Christ helps us with this. He is the admonisher, the listener, in us, the Inner Helper and Advisor. His light, His Redeemer-power, can make even the most stubborn ego-chunks melt—but we, the person, have to want this and work on ourselves accordingly.

Jesus, the Christ, teaches us the inner religion, the becoming one with the Spirit, which is within each one of us. The church denominations taught and teach that the human being is there for religion. But religion is there for the human being.

The inner religion is the religion of joy, not that of fear of sin. Sin can be overcome with Christ.

For this reason, do not be afraid of sin! Sacrifice your wrong thoughts on the inner altar. Thus, sacrifice your sins and believe in Jesus, the Christ, by doing what He taught us. Then you will become more joyful, hopeful and confident. You will attain steadfastness and security in Christ.

Jesus taught us the inner religion with very simple words. He also taught us the following words that God gave through Moses: *You shall love the Lord, your God, with all your heart and soul and with all your strength.* And: *You shall love your neighbor as yourself.*

This sentence contains all of life. Those who strive for this high goal in life begin to follow Jesus. They need no outer religion, no church denomination; they are disciples of Jesus, because they do what Jesus wants.

Let go of egoistic, dishonest thinking! Become a conscientious, honest person in your entire behavior; then you will attain resurrection in Christ.

No outer religion is needed for this and no theological, elaborate arts for religion. It is not theological studies or the intellect that make you a Christian; nor do regulations and rituals make you Christian, but it is solely the active faith that fills your heart and gives you the certainty that the Christ of God dwells in you and guides you.

Believe firmly that God helps. We human beings are children of our eternal Father, who loves us and wants to give us everything. He wants to make our heart rich.

For this reason, we should not always beg God in prayer for this or that, but should thank Him more often, even in suffering, in joyless hours, in depression, illness and in hours of loneliness. Let us thank Him, because everything that happens to us as pain, suffering, illness, need and loneliness was and is our wrong way of behaving. Those who thank God, and do this from their heart, can be sure that God helps as it is good for their soul. Pray to God with a fulfilled and trusting heart. In time, deep prayer will give you security and hold.

Every person has good and less good sides. The one who holds on to the good will have sunnier days. Seek first the Kingdom of God and His righteousness every day—no matter what happens to you or whom you meet—then the Kingdom of God, the love and kindness, will also rise and grow in your heart. Then your worries will melt away like wax in the sun.

Remember: *You* bear the responsibility for your life on Earth, and no other. The course of your earthly existence is determined by the content of your feeling, sensing, thinking, speaking and acting.

Every evening make an honest self-examination and you will gradually learn who you really are. With this, you can also figure out aspects of your subconscious, which gives you orders that you have carried out until now without recognizing this. Through this self-examination, you look behind your thoughts and words and experience their content.

Those who declare war on their base nature and are victorious over it with the help of the Spirit of God show their true face, because they no longer need their mask and their masquerade. They have become straightforward, honest and sincere.

If you would like to, think about the following:

When we meet people and they look at us, each one of us is exposed to critical eyes and possibly to critical thoughts. It is seldom that two people are in agreement. People who let the Spirit, God, resurrect in them benevolently withstand critical eyes and thinking.

Those who do not withstand criticism feel uncomfortable in their stomach area; this means they are affected. This shows that the critical one has stirred correspondences in the affected one. Those who think about what lies behind their consternation and find the cause within themselves have found a part of their egotistical self. New paths reveal themselves to the one who accepts sincere criticism.

Who was and is your best teacher? Is it the person who has admired and admires you, who spoke and speaks according to your cast of mind, who flattered and flatters you, who never criticized or criticizes you, who confirms you, even builds you up, in everything you say and do? Or have you learned more from the people who criticize you, who perhaps rejected and reject you, that is, who do not like you and exclude you from their lives? Therefore, who was and is the best teacher?

If you want to take your life in hand and shape it positively, then become your personal critic, by questioning what you think, what you say about your fellow people and how you behave toward them more and more often and by questioning yourself through self-analysis. Every self-deception is a noose that goes around your neck and at some point, will be tightened or even pulled completely tight by the law of sowing and reaping.

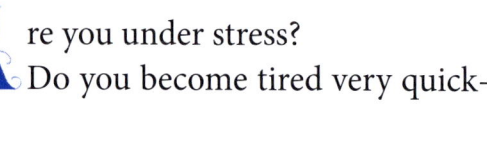Are you under stress?

Do you become tired very quickly?

Have you already noticed that stress and being hectic cause nervous tension?

That nervous tension leads, in turn, to an overstrained nervous system and to an abnormal fatigue?

Have you already ascertained that an overtaxed nervous system affects one's sight and hearing?

Then ask yourself what you want to do against this. If you would like to, turn at random to another page in the book *Open up and Find Yourself. The Treasure Chest of My Existence.* Perhaps you will receive further help in the statements you find there.

Many people work only with their heads, in the belief that the intellect is the be all and end all, instead of realizing that the All-wisdom of infinity is in the very basis of the soul of each individual and that the All-wisdom, the eternal cosmic law, knows about all things.

If you have learned to entrust yourself to the eternal all-cosmic wisdom, you work with your head and your heart. Then you work much more consciously. This communicative way of working loosens the tension in your body and raises your performance.

Communicative relaxation, in order to think and work purposefully, can take place as follows:
Relax several times a day. Sit down upright on a chair. Place both feet on the floor. Place the backs of your hands on your thighs. Close your eyes. Turn your senses to within.

Affirm the All-wisdom of infinity, the source of all knowledge and all power. Entrust yourself to God. In your inner being, address Christ, the Inner Helper and Advisor, the eternal Spirit, who is everything in all things and in every one, the power and the salvation, the great kindness and friendliness. Immerse in your prayer thoughts or in the words of your prayer that are spoken out loud. In this way, you attain the connection with the great, helping, all-wise Spirit in you.

After your prayer, remain sitting quietly for a few minutes. Do not allow any thoughts in and inhale and exhale deeply. When inhaling, let your breath stream harmoniously into your abdomen, then exhale slowly and consciously.

Thus, you breathe in consciously and breathe out consciously.
In this way, you breathe out of your body the tensions that may still be in you.
Therefore, inhale and exhale deeply several times.
Then let it breathe by letting your breath come and go, just as it corresponds to your body rhythm.

Stay in your normal breathing rhythm for a few more minutes before continuing with your work.

If you pause several times a day for a few minutes, in order to pray and to breathe consciously, you will soon sense that you relax more each time.

The evening of a day reaches out to the morning.

After your day's work, do not simply say: "The day is over" or "I have managed to do my work."

Each evening ask yourself how you have lived your day, how you have done your work and how it was for your fellow people.

The trained self-observer is alert.

Those who are a good self-observer notice in time when they begin to brood about situations, things, problems and worries. They will then take a pause and immediately question themselves, for they know that brooding merely intensifies the evil.

Those who take it as a task to get to the bottom of what wants to preoccupy them in thoughts and feelings, of what robs them of worktime and life force will recognize these signs in time, and will tackle and solve the difficulty right away. However, those who put it off will brood for days and weeks, thus intensifying their problems and worries, which rob time and drain life force.

For many a one, this putting-things-off can lead to a crooked track that goes downward.

The one who is willing to learn each day wins!

Those who want to assume a responsible position in their occupation, first learn to plan in the right way, to purposefully run through and organize the hours, the days, weeks and possibly the months. They also learn to delegate conscientiously and to supervise what they have initiated. They do not let it out of their awareness until it is finished.

Everything is energy.

Make yourself aware over and over again that wherever your thoughts go, it is there that your energies collect. If you are low in energy, think about the following: Impure, spiteful, envious, quarrelsome thoughts draw to the same kinds of energies, gather these up and bring even more such tormenting spirits in their wake. These rob the impure thinker of more energy. The results are weariness, nervousness and an unhealthy exhaustion. Many a one then asks himself: "Where has my energy gone to?"

A help for self-observation: Our life on Earth and the life of our soul after the death of our body are the product of our thoughts.

Whether we perform well on our job depends on our thoughts.

Whether we sleep well and peacefully during the night or not, we decide ourselves—through our thoughts.

Think upon the law of attraction:
Today you are afraid of what could happen. Tomorrow it will happen. What we are afraid of is what we attract.

Our whole earthly existence consists of learning.
If you learn to look at your fears and worries from a distance, you will see more and can also rectify them more easily.

Who can ruin your day? Only you, yourself!

When you are tempted to disassociate yourself from your fellow people, because they—as you believe—ruin your day, then a piece of advice: Hang in there! Your fellow people endured you yesterday—endure them today. Leave what will be tomorrow to God.

Remember: God is with the one who changes for the positive and perseveres. Only cowards who want to use their fellow people for their own purposes become hypocrites. They disassociate themselves from their fellow people and turn their back on them when they are no longer servile to them and no longer submissive.

A piece of advice for becoming happy:
Expect much, yes, everything, from yourself, but nothing from your fellow people. Then you can live with them.

H elp for self-help:
When you are depressed, work out physically. If you get really tired from this and can sleep deeply, then often you have already slept away your depression. However, if it should come again, this indicates that you are being pressured by your subconscious to find the root of the depression. This means to analyze the depressive thoughts in order to remove them from the basis of the soul and the

subconscious. Once you have largely rectified the causes, you may be sure that the sun will shine again.

Do not take yourself so seriously, then it will be possible for you to quickly gain the upper hand over what flies at you as negativity.

Despite analysis and self-recognition, many a one of us has to have their own experiences. When these knock you to the ground—get up again! Then you have already brought many a thing behind you—without losing energy unnecessarily.

Learn to be just and honest in all things to yourself and to your fellow people. Then you can say with certainty: God takes care of you.

Justice and honesty contain the reward from heaven. Injustice and dishonesty bring only difficulties, problems and misfortune into your earthly existence.

Pray a lot!

Speak to God in prayer. Although He knows about our difficulties and problems, we should tell them to Him.
If it is possible for you, speak to God out loud. Speak from within your worries and problems, your sorrow, your inferiority complexes and strive to find your next positive steps in the Ten Commandments of God and in the Sermon on the Mount of Jesus.

God is in you. Turn to Him. Christ is waiting in the very basis of your soul for you to entrust yourself to Him. He is dependable.
Take this path, and you will very gradually experience God in your heart and in your neighbor.

Prayer, which should be without expectation, gives you the strength to master each day. Then you will soon experience that each day is an aspect of the inner resurrection and that each new day is a gift from God, in order to work on the resurrection, which is the path into peace, into happiness, into secureness and security.

This is the path to freedom, to the Kingdom of God, which is within you.

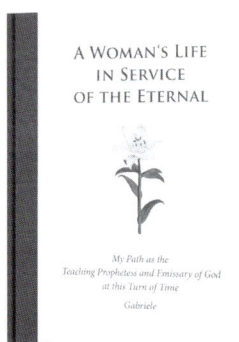

A Woman's Life in Service of the Eternal

My Path as the Teaching Prophetess and Emissary of God at this Turn of Time

Gabriele

For over 45 years now, Gabriele has been serving God, the Eternal, as His prophetess and emissary. In her autobiographical descriptions, she gives a lively insight into her development as a human being and her calling to be the prophetess of God—and what it means to bring to the Earth in our time the word of God, His love and wisdom.

With this book you hold a jewel in your hands. It contains the autobiographical memories of Gabriele, who completely devoted her whole life to God and accomplished indescribably great things for Him, for us people and for creation.

204 pp., HB, Order No. S 551en,
ISBN: 978-3-89201-814-8

The Soul on Its Path to Perfection

Through Gabriele, the prophetess and emissary of God in our time, the Christ of God reveals details about the makeup of the creation of the Being and of our soul.

Christ extensively explains the seven levels of consciousness of the soul—from Order, and via Will, to Wisdom, Earnestness, all the way to Patience, Love and Mercy. To activate these levels of the soul is the task of every soul—here on Earth or in the spheres of the beyond. These explanations from the Kingdom of God serve to uplift us and, above all, serve the maturation of the soul.

116 pp., HB, Order No. S 209en,
ISBN: 978-3-89201-952-7

Live the Moment

and You Will See and Know Yourself

Each day brings to each person what is significant for them today, at every moment.

As Gabriele explains: *At every moment, the sensations and thoughts that concern a person's spiritual and physical situation flash through their mind. They want to either give warning or show new ways … or guide the person correctly in a situation.*

This books opens our eyes, showing us how we can set the course for our future at every moment.

100 pp., SB, Order No. S 315en,
ISBN: 978-3-96446-222-0

Gabriele Publishing House – The Word
P.O. Box 2221, Deering, NH 03244, USA
Toll-free Orders: 1-844-576-0937
International Orders: +49.9391.504-843
www.Gabriele-Publishing-House.com